My Little Book of
SALVATION

Glen Wilson

InfusedMedia Co. LLC
www.infusedmedia.co
1-888-251-6088

FORWARD

This **Little Book of Salvation** just the beginning of salvation. I began this race over thirty years ago. Over the years, I have had some pastors I liked. Some disappointed me. There has been more pastors over the years than I can remember. Oddly enough, not one of them told me the only name that means, victory, salvation, and deliverance. They had no idea of how to explain the questions I had. I know there will be words in this book that you have never seen or heard before. I have two other books available. www.amazon.com, www.barnsandnoble.com, www.xlibris.com

And most other book store web sites. They are "My Person Book Of YahUwah" Study Guide with the New Testament, and the Study Guide #1.

BACKGROUND CHECK

Every since the day I was born, I was told what to believe and do. Asking questions was taboo. I went to church almost every Sunday. I sat on the pews and listened to what they had to say. Most of the time, the things I was told to do were not the actions of those telling me to do them. Actions speak louder than words, to me. At the age of forty years old, I decided to do an in depth background check on the reality of those I had been taught to believe in. I was told to pray to Jesus Christ, God the Father, and ask the LORD to forgive my sins.

First of all, I looked up the name Jesus in the Greek New Testament dictionary and it reads, "Iesous, ***ee-ay-sooce***'; of Hebrew [3091]; Jesus i.e.Joshua." This sounded very wrong to me so I kept digging. I came to find out Iesous is a Egyptian sun idol, the son of the Egyptian sun idol Zeus. Iesous had a sister, the Egyptian sun idol Isis, the Egyptian sun idol of Healing. She is also Iesous' wife. I know, this is all Greek to me too. You may be more familiar with the winged horse of Zeus, "Pegasus." I know that in Spanish the name Jesus is pronounced ***"Hay-SOOS."*** and in Hebrew it is pronounced "a soos" which translates to English as "a horse." As used in Psalm 33:17 "**An horse*(i.e. a soos)*** is a vain thingfor safety:"

Secondly, I looked up the word Christ in Greek, and it said, "Christos from 5548; anointed, i.e. the Messiah. Well, Christos is the same word in Spanish, but Christos is shortened for the Egyptian sun idol "Christos Helios. Translated to English it means "Christ the true sun." It has been ten years since I first learned this information. And it still makes me sick to my stomach. It is beginning to sound like the very leaders I trusted in have deceived me and all the millions of people that has been taught these lies. But my background check was not finished yet.

Thirdly, I looked up the word "God" in the Greek dictionary, it reads, Theos of un-serenity; a deity. Come to find out he is the name of another sun idol. When I read this verses, in the Scripture it all began to make sense to me,

Isaiah 46:5-6 "To whom will ye liken me, and make me equal, and compare me, that we may be like?

6 They lavish **gold** out of the bag, and weigh silver in the balance, and hire a **goldsmith**; and he maketh it a **god** _(note! "Gold" - minus "l" = equals god)_: they fall down, yea, they worship."

The Webster's New Collegiate Dictionary says that the origin of the word "god" comes from a Germanic word "gad," pronounced as "gohdt." Gad was one of the son's of Jacob, who was renamed Israel. The name Gad means Wealthy; however, no matter how you pronounce it, it still remains a graven image.

Finally I got to the "LORD" in the Greek it said, "Kurios from Kuros; supreme in authority, i.e. controller; by implying Mr. (As a respectful title):- God, Lord, master, sir." Kurios is just the name of another sun idol. Then, I realized we went to church on Sunday, the day they worship the sun idols. I had looked up the names; Jesus, Christ, God, and the Lord. I Came to find out, "I had all strikes, and no balls." I felt defeated. My heart had sunk in my chest. But then I realized, "I had no balls." Then, when I found these verses, I began to understand why everyone I knew was living in lies.

Jeremiah 23:26-27 "How long shall this be in the heart of the prophets that prophesy lies? yea, they are prophets of the deceit of their own heart;

27 Which think to cause my people to forget my name by their dreams which they tell every man to his neighbour, as their fathers have forgotten my name forBaal."

When I looked up the name "Baal" in the dictionary it means; master, owner, **"the Lord."** Baal is the male fertility sex idol they worship on Sunday. So, when your pastor greets you this Sunday, and says, welcome to the house of "the Lord", this beautiful day of "The Lord." You will know he is referring to the male fertility sex idol "Baal."

When I had looked up the word Jesus, it said, Joshua from Hebrew word 3091 Hebrew word "YahUshua". So I realized that I needed to see this word in the Scriptures, with my own eyes.

Exodus 14:13 "And Moses said unto the people, Fear ye not, stand still, and see the **salvation***(i.e. yshuw'ah)*of..."

Exodus 23:20-21 "Behold, I send a Messenger before thee, to keep thee in the way, and to bring thee into the place which I have prepared.

21 Beware of him, and obey his voice, provoke him not; for he will not pardon your transgressions: for my name is in him."

When I saw the word "salvation, it reminded me of the verse in the New Testament when the Jewish priest was preparing to circumcise the baby.

Luke 2:30-31 "For mine eyes have seen thy **salvation**,

31 Which thou hast prepared before the face of all people;"

I realized the word Salvation was also the name YAHUSHUA. In my own mind, this seemed like it was something that I was beginning to understand.

Second of all, when the Samaritan lady was speaking to the savourat the well. She had said,

John 4:25 "The woman saith unto him, I know that Messias cometh..." Then I thought to myself, "what does the word Messias mean?

So, I looked it up too and it said from Hebrew word 4899. I came to find out it means, "a consecrated person of YAH." YAH was a word I did recognize. It comes from the word Hallelujah, and can be found in the Scriptures. Psalm 68:4 "... sing praises to his name extol him that rideth upon the heavens by his name JAH, and rejoice before him." So I looked up the word "JAH." it said it was pronounced "YAHH" with two letters "H" in it. "Messiah "a concreted person of **YAH** makes a lot more since than the name of Christos a sun idol.

Thirdly, I had discovered the truth and the word "God." In **Matthew 1:23** "Behold, a virgin shall be with child, and shall bring forth a son, and they shall call his name Emmanuel, which being interpreted is God with us."

Well, I had already found out that a "god" was a graven image of gold. So, I looked up the word in the old Testament. "Immanuel" it is found in Isaiah 7:14. I found out that Hebrew reads from right to left. The word "Immanuel means Elohim hides among us. The word Elohim is a Hebrew word which means "His Majesty." So Emanuel was the original undercover boss.

Fourth of all, if I was to prove the information I had found I needed to find the name of the father in the son's name YahUshua? I had seen the name Jehovah in the Scriptures. But it did not have the son's name in it. So I looked it up. There was no letter "J" five-hundred years ago. But the word **YAH** is Hebrew it means Self existent or eternal. And the word hovah means; lazy, worthless, and deceitful. Then, I wrote the word JEHOVAH on a piece of paper. OK, there was no letter J five hundred years ago. So, the JEH became a YAHH, and the second letter H and the letter O becomes the Hebrew vowel point "U" in Hebrew meaning (is) and the letter "V" did not exist in ancient Hebrew. So the word JEHOVAH becomes YahUwah. We read in Exodus 23:21 He said my name is in him. Do you see the name of YahUwah in the son's Hebrew name **"YahshUwah"**?Hallelujah there it is in big bold letters. His name means long form **YAH** (is) breath or life, or short form Eternal life. While the son's name means **YAH** (is) salvation, or simply eternal Salvation.

This has been an interesting journey.I was once blind to the truth, but now I can clearly see. YahUshua the Messiah. Elohim His Majesty, The Father's name is YahUwah.

Proverbs 30:4, 8-9 "Who hath ascended up into heaven, or descended? who hath gathered the wind in his fists? who hath bound the waters in a garment? who hath established all the ends of the earth? what is his name, and what is his son's name, if thou canst tell?

8 Remove far from me vanity and lies: give me neither poverty nor riches; feed me with food convenient for me:

9 Lest I be full, and deny thee, and say, Who is**YahUwah**? or lest I be poor, and steal, and take the name of my **Elohim** in vain."

Jeremiah 16:19-21 "O **YahUwah**, my strength, and my fortress, and my refuge in the day of affliction, the Gentiles shall come unto thee from the ends of the earth, and shall say, Surely our fathers have inherited lies, vanity, and things wherein there is no profit.

20 Shall a man make elohims unto himself, and they are no elohims?

21 Therefore, behold, I will this once cause them to know, I will cause them to know mine hand and my might; and they shall know that my name is **YahUwah.**"

1 Corinthians 12:1-2 "Now concerning spiritual gifts, brethren, I would not have you ignorant.

2 Ye know that ye were Gentiles, carried away unto these dumb idols, even as ye were led.
"

John 5:42-43 "But I know you, that ye have not the love of **Elohim** in you.

43 I am come in my Father's name, and ye receive me not: if another shall come in his own name, him ye will receive."

Acts 2:36 Therefore let all the house of Israel know assuredly, that **Elohim** hath made the same **YahUshua**, whom ye have stauroo, both **YahUwah** and **Messiah** *(i.e. concentrated person of Yah)*.

John 13:13 Ye call me Master and **YahUwah**: and ye say well; for so I am.

THE A, B, C'S OF SALVATION

Admit that you are a sinner.

Romans 6:18, 23 Being then made free from sin, ye became the servants of righteousness.

23 For the wages of sin is death; but the gift of **Elohim** is eternal life through YahUshua the **Messiah** our YahUwah.

Believe on His Name

John 1:11, 12 He came unto his own, and his own received him not.

12 But as many as received him, to them gave he power to become the sons of **Elohim**, even to them that believeon his name:

John 5:42, 43 But I know you, that ye have not the love of **Elohim** in you.

43 I am come in my Father's name, and ye receive me not: if another shall come in his **own***(i.e. Jesus)*name, him ye will receive.

Confess your sins.

Romans 10:9, 10 That if thou shalt confess with thy mouth YahUwahYahUshua, and shalt believe in thine heart that **Elohim** hath raised him from the dead, thou shalt be saved.

10 For with the heart man believeth unto righteousness; and with the mouth confession is made unto salvation.

Romans 15:9, 10 And that the Gentiles might magnify **Elohim** for his mercy; as it is written, For this cause I will confess to thee among the Gentiles, and sing unto thy name.

10 And again he saith, Rejoice, ye Gentiles, with his people.

Salvation

Acts 4:12, 13 Neither is there salvation in any other: for there is none other name under heaven given among men, whereby we must be saved.

13 Now when they saw the boldness of Peter and John, and perceived that they were unlearned and ignorant men, they marvelled; and they took knowledge of them, that they had been with **YahUshua**.

Ecclesiastes 12:12-13 And further, by these, my son,

be admonished: of making many books there is no end; and much study is a weariness of the flesh.

13 Let us hear the conclusion of the whole matter: **Fear _(i.e. reverence)_Elohim**, and keep his commandments: for this is the whole duty of man.

Exodus 3:13-15 And Moses said unto **Elohim**, Behold, when I come unto the children of Israel, and shall say unto them, **Elohim** of your fathers hath sent me unto you; and they shall say to me, What is his name? what shall I say unto them?

14 And **Elohim** said unto Moses, I **AM**_(hayah i.e. to exist)_THAT I **AM**_(hayah i.e. to exist)_: and he said, Thus shalt thou say unto the children of Israel, I **AM**_(i.e.hayah)_ THAT I **AM**_(hayah i.e. to exist)_ hath **AM** _(i.e.hayah)_sent me unto you.

15 And **Elohim** said moreover unto Moses, Thus shalt thou say unto the children of Israel, **YahUwah** the **Elohim** of your fathers, the **Elohim** of Abraham,the **Elohim** of Isaac, andthe **Elohim** of Jacob, hath sent me unto you: this is my name for ever, and this is my memorial unto all generations.

HIDDEN IN MY HEART

Psalm 119:10-15 With my whole heart have I sought thee: O let me not wander from thy commandments.

11 Thy word have I **hid** _(i.e. protect, treasured)_ in mine heart, that I might not sin against thee.

12 Blessed art thou, O **YahUwah**: teach me thy statutes.

13 With my lips have I declared all the judgments of thy mouth.

14 I have rejoiced in the way of thy testimonies, as much as in all riches.

15 I will meditate in thy precepts, and have respect unto thy ways.

Psalm 37:25-31 I have been young, and now am old; yet have I not seen the righteous forsaken, nor his seed begging bread.

26 He is ever merciful, and lendeth; and his seed is blessed.

27 Depart from evil, and do good; and dwell for evermore.

28 For **YahUwah** loveth judgment, and forsaketh not his saints; they are preserved for ever: but the seed of the wicked shall be cut off.

29 The righteous shall inherit the land, and dwell therein for ever.

30 The mouth of the righteous speaketh wisdom, and his tongue talketh of judgment.

31 The law of his **Elohim** is in his heart; none of his steps shall slide.

The mouth gives evidence of one's character.

Deuteronomy 6:3-9 Hear therefore, O Israel, and observe to do it; that it may be well with thee, and that ye may increase mightily, as YahUwahElohim of thy fathers hath promised thee, in the land that floweth with milk and honey.

4 Hear, O Israel: YahUwah our **Elohim** is one YahUwah:

5 And thou shalt **love***(i.e. 'ahab)*YahUwah thy **Elohim** with all thine heart, and with all thy soul, and with all thy might.

6 And these words, which I command thee this day, shall be in thine heart:

7 And thou shalt teach them diligently unto thy children, and shalt talk of them when thou sittest in thine house, and when thou walkest by the way, and when thou liest down, and when thou risest up.

8 And thou shalt bind them for a sign upon thine hand,
and they shall be as frontlets between thine eyes.

9 And thou shalt write them upon the posts of thy house, and on thy gates.

Psalm 40:1-8 I waited patiently for YahUwah; and he inclined unto me, and heard my cry. 2 He brought me up also out of an horrible pit, out of the miry clay, and set my feet upon a rock, and established my goings.

3 And he hath put a new song in my mouth, even praise unto our **Elohim**: many shall see it, and fear, and shall trust in YahUwah.

4 Blessed is that man that maketh YahUwah his trust, and respecteth not the proud, nor such as turn aside to lies.

5 Many, O YahUwah my **Elohim**, are thy wonderful works which thou hast done, and thy thoughts which are to us-ward: they cannot be reckoned up in order unto thee: if I would declare and speak of them, they are more than can be numbered.

6 atonements and offering thou didst not desire; mine ears hast thou opened: burnt offering and sin offering hast thou not required.

7 Then said I, Lo, I come: in the volume of the book it is written of me,

8 I delight to do thy will, O my **Elohim**: yea, thy law is within my heart.

Psalm 119:97-104 O how **love** *(i.e. ahab; to have affection sexually or otherwise)*I thy law! it is my meditation all the day.

98 Thou through thy commandments hast made me wiser than mine enemies: for they are ever with me.

99 I have more understanding than all my teachers: for thy testimonies are my meditation.

100 I understand more than the ancients, because I keep thy precepts.

101 I have refrained my feet from every evil way, that I might keep thy word.

102 I have not departed from thy judgments: for thou hast taught me.

103 How sweet are thy words unto my taste! yea, sweeter than honey to my mouth!

104 Through thy precepts I get understanding: therefore I hate every false way.

Isaiah 51:5-6 My righteousness is near; my **salvation***(i.e. yesha)* is gone forth, and mine arms shall judge the people; the isles shall wait upon me, and on mine arm shall they trust.

6 Lift up your eyes to the heavens, and look upon the earth beneath: for the heavens shall vanish away like smoke, and the earth shall wax old like a garment, and they that dwell therein shall die in like manner: but my **salvation***(i.e. yshuw'ah)* shall be for ever, and my righteousness shall not be abolished.

MEMORY VERSES

Exodus 3:15 And **Elohim** said moreover unto Moses, Thus shalt thou say unto the children of Israel, Y{\sc ah}U{\sc wah}**Elohim** of your fathers, the **Elohim** of Abraham, the **Elohim** of Isaac, and the **Elohim** of Jacob, hath sent me unto you: this is my name for ever, and this is my memorial unto all generations.

Exodus 9:16 And in very deed for this cause have I raised thee up, for to shew in thee my power; and that my name may be declared throughout all the earth.

Exodus 20:3-6 Thou shalt have no **other _(i.e. strange)_**elohims before me.

4 Thou shalt not make unto thee any graven image, or any likeness of any thing that is in heaven above, or that is in the earth beneath, or that is in the water under the earth.

5 Thou shalt not bow down thyself to them, nor serve them: for I Y{\sc ah}U{\sc wah} thy **Elohim** am a jealous **El**, visiting the iniquity of the fathers upon the children unto the third and fourth generation of them that hate me;

6 And shewing mercy unto thousands of them that love me, and keep my commandments.

Exodus 23:13 And in all things that I have said unto you be circumspect: and make no mention of the name of other _(i.e. strange)_ elohims, neither let it be heard out of thy mouth.

Exodus 31:15 Six days may work be done; but in the seventh is the sabbath of rest, kodesh to **YahUwah**: whosoever doeth any work in the sabbath day, he shall surely be put to death.

Leviticus 11:7-8 And the swine, though he divide the hoof, and be cloven-footed, yet he cheweth not the cud; he is unclean to you.

8 Of their flesh shall ye not eat, and their carcase shall ye not touch; they are unclean to you.

Leviticus 26:2-5 Ye shall keep my sabbaths, and reverence my kodesh-place: I am **YahUwah**.

3 If ye walk in my statutes, and keep my commandments, and do them;

4 Then I will give you rain in due season, and the land shall yield her increase, and the trees of the field shall yield their fruit.

5 And your threshing shall reach unto the vintage, and the vintage shall reach unto the sowing time: and ye shall eat your bread to the full, and dwell in your land safely.

Numbers 15:37-40 And **YahUwah** spake unto Moses, saying, 38 Speak unto the children of Israel, and bid them that they make them fringes in the borders of their garments throughout their generations, and that they put upon the fringe of the borders a ribband of blue:

39 And it shall be unto you for a fringe, that ye may look upon it, and remember all the commandments of **YahUwah**, and do them; and that ye seek not after your own heart and your own eyes, after which ye use to go a whoring:

40 That ye may remember, and do all mycommandments, and be kodesh unto your **Elohim**.

Deuteronomy 4:27-29 And **YahUwah** shall scatter you among the nations, and ye shall be left few in number among the heathen, whither **YahUwah**shall lead you.

28 And there ye shall serve **idols** *(see Jer. 16:13; Ps. 115:4-7; Ps. 135:15-17)*, the work of men's hands, wood and stone, which neither see, nor hear, nor eat, nor smell.

29 But if from thence thou shalt seek Y**ah**U**wah** thy **Elohim**, thou shalt find him, if thou seek him with all thy heart and with all thy soul.

Deuteronomy 6:13-14 Thou shalt **fear** *(i.e. reverence)* Y**ah**U**wah** thy **Elohim**, and serve him, and shalt **swear** *(i.e. take an oath)*by his name.

14 Ye shall not go after **other** *(i.e. strange)*elohims, of the elohims of the people which are round about you;

Deuteronomy 13:3-4 Thou shalt not hearken unto the words of that prophet, or that dreamer of dreams: for Y**ah**U**wah** your **Elohim**proveth you, to know whether ye love Y**ah**U**wah** your **Elohim** with all your heart and with all your soul.

4 Ye shall walk after Y**ah**U**wah**your **Elohim**, and **fear** *(i.e. reference)*him, and keep his commandments, and obey his voice, and ye shall serve him, and cleave unto him.

Deuteronomy 28:58 If thou wilt not observe to do all the words of this law that are written in this book, that thou mayest **fear***(i.e. reverence)*this magnificent and fearful name, Y**ah**U**wah** Thy **Elohim**;

Deuteronomy 32:1-3 Give ear, O ye heavens, and I will speak; and hear, O earth, the words of my mouth.

2 My doctrine shall drop as the rain, my speech shall distil as the dew, as the small rain upon the tender herb, and as the showers upon the grass:

3 Because I will publish the name of Yah**U**wah**: ascribe ye greatness unto our Elohim.**

Joshua 23:7-8 That ye come not among these nations, these that remain among you; neither make mention of the name of their elohims, nor cause to swear by them, neither serve them, nor bow yourselves unto them:8 But **cleave** *(i.e. purse hard)*unto Y**ah**U**wah** your **Elohim**, as ye have done unto this day.

Judges 2:11-13 And the children of Israel did evil in the sight of Y**ah**U**wah**, and served **Baalim** *(i.e. the lords)*:

12 And they forsook **YahUwahElohim** of their fathers, which brought them out of the land of Egypt, and followed **other***(i.e. strange)* elohims, of the elohims of the people that were round about them, and bowed themselves unto them, and provoked **YahUwah** to anger.

13 And they forsook **YahUwah**, and served **Baal***(i.e. the lord)* and Ashtaroth.

1 Kings 8:43-44 Hear thou in heaven thy dwelling place, and do according to all that the stranger calleth to thee for: that all people of the earth may know thy name, to **fear** *(i.e. reverence)* thee, as do thy people Israel; and that they may know that this house, which I have builded, is called by thy name.

44 If thy people go out to battle against their enemy, whithersoever thou shalt send them, and shall pray unto **YahUwah** toward the city which thou hast chosen, and toward the house that I have built for thy name:

1 Chronicles 16:8-10 Give thanks unto **YahUwah**, call upon his name, make known his deeds among the people.

9 Sing unto him, sing psalms unto him, talk ye of all his wondrous works.

10 Honor ye in his kodesh name: let the heart of them rejoice that seek **YahUwah**.

1 Chronicles 16:25, 29 For great is **YahUwah**, and greatly to be praised: he also is to be feared above all elohims.

29 Give unto **YahUwah** the honor due unto his name: bring an offering, and come before him: worship **YahUwah**in the beauty of kodeshness.

1 Chronicles 17:24 Let it even be established, that thy name may be magnified for ever, saying, **YahUwah** of hosts is the **Elohim** of Israel, even a**Elohim** to Israel: and let the house of David thy servant be established before thee.

1 Chronicles 28:7-8 Moreover I will establish his kingdom for ever, if he be constant to do my commandments and my judgments, as at this day.

8 Now therefore in the sight of all Israel the congregation of **YahUwah**, and in the audience of our **Elohim**, keep and seek for all

the commandments of YahUwah your **Elohim**: that ye may possess this good land, and leave it for an inheritance for your children after you for ever.

Joshua 24:13-16 And I have given you a land for which ye did not labour, and cities which ye built not, and ye dwell in them; of the vineyards and oliveyards which ye planted not do ye eat. 14 Now therefore **fear** *(i.e. reverence)*YahUwah, and serve him in sincerity and in truth: and put away the elohims which your fathers served on the other side of the flood, and in Egypt; and serve ye YahUwah.

15 And if it seem evil unto you to serve YahUwah, choose you this day whom ye will serve; whether the elohims which your fathers served that were on the other side of the flood, or the elohims of the Amorites, in whose land ye dwell: but as for me and my house, we will serve YahUwah.

16 And the people answered and said, **[Elohim]** forbid that we should forsake YahUwah, to serve other elohims;

Job 28:28 And unto man he said, Behold, the **fear***(i.e. reverence)*of the **Sovereign**, that is wisdom; and to depart from evil is understanding.

Psalm 5:11 But let all those that put their trust in thee rejoice: let them ever shout for joy, because thou defendest them: let them also that **love***(i.e. ahab' like a friend)*thy name be joyful in thee.

Psalm 9:9-10 YahUwah also will be a refuge for the oppressed, a refuge in times of trouble.

10 And they that know thy name will put their trust in thee: for thou, YahUwah, hast not forsaken them that seek thee.

Psalm 10:4 The wicked, through the pride of his countenance, will not **seek***(i.e. usually to follow (for pursuit or search)*after **[Elohim]**: **Elohim** is not in all his thoughts.

Psalm 16:4 Their sorrows shall be multiplied that hasten after **another** *(i.e. strange)*[elohim]: their drink offerings of blood will I not offer, nor take up their names into my lips.

Psalm 18:30-32 As for **El**, his way is **perfect** *(i.e. complete, full, perfect)*: the word of YahUwah is tried: he is a buckler to all those that trust in him.

31 For who is **Elowahh** save YᴀʜUᴡᴀʜ? or who is a rock save our **Elohim**?

32 It is **El** that girdeth me with strength, and maketh my way **perfect** _(i.e. complete without spot)_.

Psalm 20:7 Some trust in chariots, and some in **horses**_(i.e. a soos)_: but we will remember the name of YᴀʜUᴡᴀʜ our **Elohim**.

Psalm 37:39-40 But the salvation of the righteous is of YᴀʜUᴡᴀʜ: he is their strength in the time of trouble.

40 And YᴀʜUᴡᴀʜ shall help them, and deliver them: he shall deliver them from the wicked, and save them, because they trust in him.

Psalm 45:17 I will make thy name to be remembered in all generations: therefore shall the people **praise**_(i.e. yadah; to revere or worship (with extended hands)_ thee for ever and ever.

Psalm 56:11-13 In **Elohim** have I put my trust: I will not be afraid what man can do unto me.

12 Thy vows are upon me, O **Elohim**: I will render praises unto thee.

13 For thou hast delivered my soul from death: wilt not thou deliver my feet from falling, that I may walk before **Elohim** in the light of the living?

Psalm 72:17 His name shall endure for ever: his name shall be continued as long as the sun: and men shall be blessed in him: all nations shall call him blessed.

Psalm 79:6, 9 Pour out thy wrath upon the heathen that have not known thee, and upon the kingdoms that have not called upon thy name.

9 Help us, O **Elohim** of our salvation, for the honor of thy name: and deliver us, and purge away our sins, for thy name's sake.

Psalm 83:16, 18 Fill their faces with shame; that they may seek thy name, O YᴀʜUᴡᴀʜ.

18 That men may know that thou, whose name alone is YᴀʜUᴡᴀʜ, art the most **high** _(i.e. '- elyown)_over all the earth.

Psalm 86:12 I will praise thee, O **Sovereign** my **Elohim**, with all my heart: and I will magnify thy name for evermore.

Psalm 91:14 Because he hath set his **love** _(i.e. khaw-shak' (have a) desire)_ upon me, therefore will I deliver him: I will set him on high, because he hath known my name.

Psalm 96:1-6 O sing unto Y{{ah}}Uwah a new song: sing unto Y{{ah}}Uwah, all the earth.

2 Sing unto Y{{ah}}Uwah, bless his name; shew forth his **salvation** _(i.e. yshuw'ah)_ from day to day.

3 Declare his honor among the heathen, his wonders among all people.

4 For Y{{ah}}Uwah is great, and greatly to be praised: he is to be feared above all elohims.

5 For all the elohims of the nations are idols: but Y{{ah}}Uwah made the heavens.

6 Honour and majesty are before him: strength and beauty are in his kodesh-place

Psalm 103:10-13 He hath not dealt with us after our sins; nor rewarded us according to our iniquities.

11 For as the heaven is high above the earth, so great is his mercy toward them that **fear** _(i.e. reverence)_ him.

12 As far as the east is from the west, so far hath he removed our transgressions from us.

13 Like as a father pitieth his children, so Y{{ah}}Uwah pitieth them that fear _(i.e. reverence)_ **him.**

Psalm 111:10 The **fear** _(i.e. reverence)_ of Y{{ah}}Uwah is the beginning of wisdom: a good understanding have all they that do his commandments: his **praise** _(i.e. thillah from hala a hymn:-- praise)_ endureth for **ever** _(i.e. eternity)._

Psalm 116:12-13 What shall I render unto Y{{ah}}Uwah for all his benefits toward me?

13 I will take the cup of **salvation** _(i.e. yshuw'ah),_ and call upon the name of Y{{ah}}Uwah.

Psalm 116:15-17 Precious in the sight of Y{{ah}}Uwah is the death of his saints.

16 O Y{{ah}}Uwah, truly I am thy servant; I am thy servant, and the son of thine handmaid: thou hast loosed my bonds.

17 I will offer to thee the atonement of thanksgiving, and will call upon the name of Y**ah**U**wah**.

Psalm 118:5-7 I called upon **YAH** in distress: **YAH** answered me, and set me in a large place.

6 Y**ah**U**wah** is on my side; I will not fear: what can man do unto me?

7 Y**ah**U**wah** taketh my part with them that help me: therefore shall I see my desire upon them that hate me.

Psalm 119:41-44 Let thy mercies come also unto me, O Y**ah**U**wah**, even thy **salvation*(i.e. tshuw'ah)***, according to thy word.

42 So shall I have wherewith to answer him that reproacheth me: for I trust in thy word.

43 And take not the word of truth utterly out of my mouth; for I have hope in thy judgments.

44 So shall I keep thy law continually for ever and ever.

Psalm 119:55 I have remembered thy name, O Y**ah**U**wah**, in the night, and have kept thy law.

Psalm 119:132 Look thou upon me, and be merciful unto me, as thou usest to do unto those that **love*(i.e. aw-hab'; to have affection for (sexually or otherwise)*** thy name.

Psalm 119:165-166 Great peace have they which **love*(i.e. 'ahab)*** thy law: and nothing shall **offend*(i.e. a stumbling-block, literally or figuratively (obstacle, enticement (specifically an idol), scruple):-- caused to fall, offence, X (no-)thing offered, ruin)***them.

166 Y**ah**U**wah**, I have hoped for thy **salvation*(i.e. yshuw 'ah)***, and done thy commandments

Psalm 125:1-2 They that trust in Y**ah**U**wah** shall be as mount Zion, which cannot be removed, but abideth for ever.

2 As the mountains are round about Jerusalem, so Y**ah**U**wah** is round about his people from henceforth even for ever.

Psalm 128:4 Behold, that thus shall the man be blessed that **feareth *(i.e. reverence)*** Y**ah**U**wah**.

Psalm 135:13-17 Thy name, O Yah**U**wah**, endureth for ever; and thy memorial, O Y**ah**U**wah**, throughout all generations.**

14 For **YahUwah** will judge his people, and he will repent himself concerning his servants.

15 The idols of the heathen are silver and gold, the work of men's hands.

16 They have mouths, but they speak not; eyes have they, but they see not;

17 They have ears, but they hear not; neither is there any breath in their mouths.

Psalm 145:21 My mouth shall speak the praise of **YahUwah**: and let all flesh bless his kodesh name for ever and ever.

Proverbs 1:7 The **fear*(i.e. reverence)*** of **YahUwah** is the beginning of knowledge: but fools despise wisdom and **instruction*(i.e. correction, rebuke)***.

Proverbs 1:28, 29 Then shall they call upon me, but I will not answer; they shall seek me early, but they shall not find me:

29 For that they hated knowledge, and did not choose the **fear*(i.e. reverence)***of **YahUwah**:

Proverbs 16:18-20 Pride goeth before destruction, and an haughty spirit before a fall.

19 Better it is to be of an humble spirit with the lowly, than to divide the spoil with the proud.

20 He that handleth a matter wisely shall find good: and whoso trusteth in **YahUwah**, happy is he.

Proverbs 18:10 The name of **YahUwah** is a strong tower: the righteous runneth into it, and is safe.

Proverbs 30:4 Who hath ascended up into heaven, or descended? who hath gathered the wind in his fists? who hath bound the waters in a garment? who hath established all the ends of the earth? what is his name, and what is his son's name, if thou canst tell?

Proverbs 30:8-9 Remove far from me **vanity *(i.e. uselessness)***and lies: give me neither poverty nor riches; feed me with food convenient for me:

9 Lest I be full, and deny thee, and say, Who is **YahUwah**? or lest I be poor, and steal, and take the name of my **Elohim** in vain.

Song of Solomon 1:3 Because of the savour of thy good ointments thy name is as **ointment** *(i.e. oil)*poured forth, therefore do the virgins **love***(i.e. aw-hab'; to have affection for (sexually or otherwise)*thee.

Matthew 25:1-13 Then shall the kingdom of heaven be likened unto ten virgins, which took their lamps, and went forth to meet the bridegroom. 2 And five of them were wise, and five were foolish.

3 They that were foolish took their lamps, and took no **oil** with them:

4 But the wise took **oil** in their vessels with their lamps.

5 While the bridegroom tarried, they all slumbered and slept.

6 And at midnight there was a cry made, Behold, the bridegroom cometh; go ye out to meet him.

7 Then all those virgins arose, and trimmed their lamps.

8 And the foolish said unto the wise, Give us of your **oil**; for our lamps are gone out.

9 But the wise answered, saying, Not so; lest there be not enough for us and you: but go ye rather to them that sell, and buy for yourselves.

10 And while they went to buy, the bridegroom came; and they that were ready went in with him to the marriage: and the door was shut.

11 Afterward came also the other virgins, saying, YᴀʜUᴡᴀʜ, YᴀʜUᴡᴀʜ, open to us.

12 But he answered and said, Verily I say unto you, I know you not.

13 Watch therefore, for ye know neither the day nor the hour wherein the Son of man cometh.

Isaiah 12:1-2 And in that day thou shalt say, O YᴀʜUᴡᴀʜ, I will praise thee: though thou wast angry with me, thine anger is turned away, and thou comfortedst me.

2 Behold, **El** is my **salvation***(i.e. yshuw'ah)*; I will trust, and not be afraid: for **YAH YᴀʜUᴡᴀʜ** is my strength and my song; he also is become my **salvation** *(i.e. yshuw'ah)*.

Isaiah 12:4 And in that day shall ye say, **Praise***(i.e. Yadah)* YᴀʜUᴡᴀʜ, call upon his name, declare his doings among the people, make mention that his name is exalted.

Isaiah 26:1-2 In that day shall this song be sung in the land of **Judah** *(i.e. Yhudah)*; We have a strong city; **salvation***(i.e. yshuw'ah)* will [**Elohim**] appoint for walls and bulwarks.

2 Open ye the gates, that the righteous **nation***(i.e. people)*which keepeth the truth may enter in.

Isaiah 26:13-14 O YᴀʜUᴡᴀʜ our **Elohim**, other masters beside thee have had dominion over us: but by thee only will we make mention of thy name.

14 They are dead, they shall not live; they are deceased, they shall not rise: therefore hast thou visited and destroyed them, and made all their memory to perish.

Isaiah 42:10-11 Ye are my witnesses, saith YᴀʜUᴡᴀʜ, and my servant whom I have chosen: that ye may know and believe me, and understand that I am he: before me there was no **El** formed, neither shall there be after me.

11 I, even I, am YᴀʜUᴡᴀʜ; and beside me there is no **saviour***(i.e. yasha')*. **Isaiah 42:8** I am YᴀʜUᴡᴀʜ: that is my name: and my honor will I not give to another, neither my praise to graven images.

Isaiah 46:6 They lavish gold out of the bag, and weigh silver in the balance, and hire a goldsmith; and he maketh it a **god***(notice "gold" - minus "l" = equals "god")*: they fall down, yea, they worship.

Isaiah 50:10 Who is among you that **feareth** *(i.e. reverence)* YᴀʜUᴡᴀʜ, that obeyeth the voice of his servant, that walketh in darkness, and hath no light? let him trust in the name of YᴀʜUᴡᴀʜ, and stay upon his **Elohim**.

Isaiah 58:9 Then shalt thou **call** *(i.e. (give) name, preach, (make) proclaim(- ation), pronounce, publish, read, renowned, say)*, and YᴀʜUᴡᴀʜshall answer; thou shalt cry, and he shall say, Here I am. If thou take away from the midst of thee the yoke, the putting forth of the finger, and speaking vanity;

Isaiah 56:5-6 Even unto them will I give in mine house and within my walls a place and a name better than of sons and of daughters: I will give them an everlasting name, that shall not be cut off.

6 Also the sons of the stranger, that join themselves to YᴀʜUᴡᴀʜ, to serve him, and to **love** *(i.e. ahab; to have affection sexually or*

otherwise) the name of **YahUwah**, to be his servants, every one that keepeth the sabbath from polluting it, and taketh hold of my covenant;

Isaiah 59:19 So shall they **fear***(i.e. reverence)*the name of **YahUwah** from the west, and his honor from the rising of the sun. When the enemy shall come in like a flood, the **Spirit***(i.e. Ruach)*of **YahUwah** shall lift up a standard against him.

Jeremiah 10:21, 25 For the pastors are become brutish, and have not sought **YahUwah**: therefore they shall not prosper, and all their flocks shall be scattered.

25 Pour out thy fury upon the heathen that know thee not, and upon the families that call not on thy name: for they have eaten up Jacob, and devoured him, and consumed him, and have made his habitation desolate.

Jeremiah 12:16 And it shall come to pass, if they will diligently learn the ways of my people, to **swear** *(i.e. take an oath)*by my name, **YahUwah** liveth; as they taught my people to swear by **Baal** *(i.e. the lord)*; then shall they be built in the midst of my people.

Jeremiah 16:19-21 O **YahUwah**, my strength, and my fortress, and my refuge in the day of affliction, the Gentiles shall come unto thee from the ends of the earth, and shall say, Surely our fathers have inherited lies, vanity, and things wherein there is no profit.

20 Shall a man make elohims unto himself, and they are no elohims?

21 Therefore, behold, I will this once cause them to know, I will cause them to know mine hand and my might; and they shall know that my name is **YahUwah**.

Jeremiah 23:27 Which think to cause my people to forget my name by their dreams which they tell every man to his neighbour, as their fathers have forgotten my name for **Baal***(i.e. the lord)*.

Jeremiah 32:18 Thou shewest lovingkindness unto thousands, and recompensest the iniquity of the fathers into the bosom of their children after them: the Great, the Mighty **El**, **YahUwah** of hosts, is his name,

Laminations 3:25-26 YahUwah is good unto them that wait for him, to the soul that seeketh him.

26 It is good that a man should both hope and quietly wait for the salvation of YahUwah.

Lamentations 3:55-57 I called upon thy name, O **YahUwah**, out of the low dungeon.

56 Thou hast heard my voice: hide not thine ear at my breathing, at my cry.

57 Thou drewest near in the day that I called upon thee: thou saidst, Fear not.

Hosea 1:7 But I will have mercy upon the house of Judah, and will save them by **YahUwah** their **Elohim**, and will not save them by bow, nor by sword, nor by battle, by **horses*(i.e. a soos)*, nor by **horsemen*(i.e. a soosmen)*.

Hosea 2:16-17 And it shall be at that day, saith **YahUwah**, that thou shalt call me **Ishi*(i.e. the man)*; and shalt call me no more **Baali *(i.e. the lord)*.

17 For I will take away the names of **Baalim*(i.e. the lords)*out of her mouth, and they shall no more be remembered by their name.

Hosea 4:1 Hear the word of **YahUwah**, ye children of Israel: for **YahUwah** hath a controversy with the inhabitants of the land, because there is no truth, nor mercy, nor knowledge of **Elohim** in the land.

Hosea 4:6 My people are destroyed for lack of knowledge: because thou hast rejected knowledge, I will also reject thee, that thou shalt be no priest to me: seeing thou hast forgotten the law of thy **Elohim**, I will also forget thy children.

Joel 2:32 And it shall come to pass, that whosoever shall call on the name of **YahUwah** shall be delivered: for in mount Zion and in Jerusalem shall be deliverance, as **YahUwah** hath said, and in the remnant whom **YahUwah** shall call.

Amos 2:4 Thus saith **YahUwah**; For three transgressions of Judah, and for four, I will not turn away the punishment thereof; because they have despised the law of **YahUwah**, and have not kept his commandments, and their **lies** caused them to **err**, after the which their fathers have walked:

Amos 8:11-12 Behold, the days come, saith the **SovereignYahUwah**, that I will send a famine in the land, not a famine of bread, nor a thirst for water, but of hearing the words of **YahUwah**:

Micah 4:5 For all people will walk every one in the name of his elohim, and we will walk in the name of **YahUwah** our **Elohim** for ever_(i.e. eternity)_and ever_(i.e. eternity)_.

Micah 6:9 YahUwah's voice crieth unto the city, and the man of wisdom shall see thy name: hear ye the rod, and who hath appointed it.

Zephaniah 3:12 I will also leave in the midst of thee an afflicted and poor people, and they shall trust in the name of **YahUwah**.

Zechariah 13:9 And I will bring the third part through the fire, and will refine them as silver is refined, and will try them as gold is tried: **they shall**

call on my name, and I will hear them: I will say, It is my people: and they shall say, **YahUwah is my Elohim**.

Malachi 2:2 If ye will not hear, and if ye will not lay it to heart, to give honor unto my name, saith **YahUwah** of hosts, I will even send a curse upon you, and I will curse your blessings: yea, I have cursed them already, because ye do not lay it to heart.

Malachi 3:16 Then they that **feared** _(i.e. reverence)_YahUwah spake often one to another: and YahUwahhearkened, and heard it, and a book of remembrance was written before him for them that **feared**_(i.e. reverenced)_YahUwah, and that **thought**_(i.e. regard, value)_ upon his name.

Malachi 4:1-2 For, behold, the day cometh, that shall burn as an oven; and all the proud, yea, and all that do wickedly, shall be stubble: and the day that cometh shall burn them up, saith **YahUwah** of hosts, that it shall leave them neither root nor branch.

2 But unto you that **fear** _(i.e. reverence)_ my name shall the Sun of righteousness arise with healing in his wings; and ye shall go forth, and grow up as calves of the stall.

Matthew 5:10-11 Blessed are they which are persecuted for righteousness' sake: for theirs is the kingdom of heaven.

11 Blessed are ye, when men shall revile you, and persecute you, and shall say all manner of evil against you falsely, for my sake.

Matthew 5:17-19 Think not that I am come to destroy the law, or the prophets: I am not come to destroy, but to fulfil.

18 For verily I say unto you, Till heaven and earth pass, one jot or one tittle shall in no wise pass from the law, till all be fulfilled.

19 Whosoever therefore shall break one of these least commandments, and shall teach men so, he shall be called the least in the kingdom of heaven: but whosoever shall do and teach them, the same shall be called great in the kingdom of heaven.

Matthew 6:25 Therefore I say unto you, Take no thought for your life, what ye shall eat, or what ye shall drink; nor yet for your body, what ye shall put on. Is not the life more than meat, and the body than raiment?

Matthew 7:22-23 Many will say to me in that day, **Lord**, **Lord** *(i.e. Baal, Baal)*, have we not prophesied in thy name? and in thy name have cast out devils? and in thy name done many wonderful works?

23 And then will I profess unto them, I never knew you: depart from me, ye that work iniquity.

Matthew 10:22-23 And ye shall be hated of all men for my name's sake: but he that endureth to the end shall be saved.

23 But when they persecute you in this city, flee ye into another: for verily I say unto you, Ye shall not have gone over the cities of Israel, till the Son of man be come.

Matthew 10:28 And **fear** *(i.e. reverence)* not them which kill the body, but are not able to kill the soul: but rather **fear** *(i.e. reverence)* him which is able to destroy both **soul** *(i.e. the rational and immortal soul)* and body in **hell** *(i.e. gheh'-en-nah, everlasting punishment)*.

Matthew 19:29 And every one that hath forsaken houses, or brethren, or sisters, or father, or mother, or wife, or children, or lands, for my name's sake, shall receive an hundredfold, and shall inherit everlasting life.

Matthew 21:9 And the multitudes that went before, and that followed, cried, saying, Hosanna to the son of David: Blessed is he that cometh in the name of **YAHUWAH**; Hosanna in the highest.

Matthew 22:36-37 Master, which is the great commandment in the law?

37 **YahUshua** said unto him, Thou shalt **love** *(i.e. agape; love, i.e. affection or benevolence)*YahUwah thy **Elohim** with all thy heart, and with all thy soul, and with all thy mind.

Matthew 23:37-39 O Jerusalem, Jerusalem, thou that killest the prophets, and stonest them which are sent unto thee, how often would I have gathered thy children together, even as a hen gathereth her chickens under her wings, and ye would not!

38 Behold, your house is left unto you desolate.

39 For I say unto you, Ye shall not see me henceforth, till ye shall say, Blessed is he that cometh in the name of **YahUwah**.

Matthew 24:9-10 Then shall they deliver you up to be afflicted, and shall kill you: and ye shall be hated of all nations for my name's sake.

10 And then shall many be offended, and shall betray one another, and shall hate one another.

Matthew 24:24-27 For there shall arise false **Messiahs***(i.e. also know as Christos)*, and false prophets, and shall shew great signs and wonders; insomuch that, if it were possible, they shall deceive the very elect.

25 Behold, I have told you before.

26 Wherefore if they shall say unto you, Behold, he is in the desert; go not forth: behold, he is in the secret chambers; believe it not.

27 For as the lightning cometh out of the east, and shineth even unto the west; so shall also the coming of the Son of man be.

Luke 9:62 And **YahUshua** said unto him, No man, having put his hand to the plough, and looking back, is fit for the kingdom of **Elohim**.

Mark 12:29-30 And **YahUshua** answered him, The first of all the commandments is, Hear, O Israel; **YahUwah**our **Elohim** is one **YahUwah**:

30 And thou shalt **love** *(i.e. agape; love, i.e. affection or benevolence)* **YahUwah** thy **Elohim** with all thy heart, and with all thy soul, and with all thy mind, and with all thy strength: this is the first commandment.

Mark 13:12-13 Now the brother shall betray the brother to death, and the father the son; and children shall rise up against their parents, and shall cause them to be put to death.

13 And ye shall be hated of all men for my name's sake: but he that shall endure unto the end, the same shall be saved.

Luke 11:52 Woe unto you, lawyers! for ye have taken away the key of knowledge: ye entered not in yourselves, and them that were entering in ye hindered.

Luke 13:24 Strive to enter in at the strait gate: for many, I say unto you, will seek to enter in, and shall not be able.

Luke 21:12 But before all these, they shall lay their hands on you, and persecute you, delivering you up to the synagogues, and into prisons, being brought before kings and rulers for my name's sake.

Luke 21:16-17 And ye shall be betrayed both by parents, and brethren, and kinsfolks, and friends; and some of you shall they cause to be put to death.

17 And ye shall be hated of all men for my name's sake.

Luke 24:47 And that repentance and remission of sins should be preached in his name among all nations, beginning at Jerusalem.

John 1:12, 14 But as many as received him, to them gave he power to become the sons of **Elohim**, even to them that believe on his name:

14 And the Word was made flesh, and dwelt among us, (and we beheld his honor, the honor as of the only begotten of the Father,) full of favor and truth.

John 3:16-18 For **Elohim** so loved the world, that he gave his only begotten Son, that whosoever believeth in him should not perish, but have everlasting life.

17 For **Elohim** sent not his Son into the world to condemn the world; but that the world through him might be saved.

18 He that believeth on him is not condemned: but he that believeth not is condemned already, because he hath not believed in the name of the only begotten Son of **Elohim**.

John 4:22-23 Ye worship ye know not what: we know what we worship: for **salvation** *(i.e. yshuw'ah)*is of the Jews.

23 But the hour cometh, and now is, when the true worshippers shall worship the Father in spirit and in truth: for the Father seeketh such to worship him.

John 5:42-43 But I know you, that ye have not the **love** *(i.e. agape)* of **Elohim** in you.

43 I am come in my Father's name, and ye receive me not: if another shall come in his own name, him ye will receive.

John 10:7-8 Then said **YAHUSHUA** unto them again, Verily, verily, I say unto you, I am the door of the sheep.

8 All that ever came before me are thieves and robbers: but the sheep did not hear them.

John 10:25YAHUSHUAanswered them, I told you, and ye believed not: the works that I do in my Father's name, they bear witness of me.

John 13:13, 14 Ye call me Master and **YAHUWAH**: and ye say well; for so I am.

14 If I then, your **YAHUWAH** and Master, have washed your feet; ye also ought to wash one another's feet.

John 14:6-7 **YAHUSHUA** saith unto him, I am the way, the truth, and the life: no man cometh unto the Father, but by me.

7 If ye had known me, ye should have known my Father also: and from henceforth ye know him, and have seen him.

John 17:6 I have manifested thy name unto the men which thou gavest me out of the world: thine they were, and thou gavest them me; and they have kept thy word.

John 17:11 And now I am no more in the world, but these are in the world, and I come to thee. Kodesh Father, keep through thine own name those whom thou hast given me, that they may be one, as we are.

John 17:26 And I have declared unto them thy name, and will declare it: that the **love** *(i.e. agape)*wherewith thou hast **loved** *(i.e. agapao)*me may be in them, and I in them.

John 20:31 But these are written, that ye might believe that YAHUSHUAis the **Messiah** *(i.e. a consecrated person of YAH)*, the Son of **Elohim**; and that believing ye might have life through his name.

John 20:29b-31 blessed are they that have not seen, and yet have believed.

30 And many other signs truly did Yah**U**shua **in the presence of his disciples, which are not written in this book: 31 But these are written, that ye might believe that Y**ah**U**shua **is the Messiah _(i.e. consecrated person of Y_**ah**_)_, the Son of Elohim; and that believing ye might have life through his name.**

Acts 2:21 And it shall come to pass, that whosoever shall call on the name of Y**ah**U**wah** shall be saved.

Acts 2:36-38 Therefore let all the house of Israel know assuredly, that **Elohim** hath made the same Y**ah**U**shua**, whom ye have stauroo, both Y**ah**U**wah** and **Messiah** _(i.e. concentrated person of Y_**ah**_)_.

37 Now when they heard this, they were pricked in their heart, and said unto Peter and to the rest of the apostles, Men and brethren, what shall we do?

38 Then Peter said unto them, Repent, and be baptized every one of you in the name of Y**ah**U**shua** the **Messiah** for the remission of sins, and ye shall receive the gift of the **Ruach Ha Kodesh** _(i.e. the set apart Spirit of Y_**ah**_U_**wah**_)_.

Acts 4:12-13 Neither is there salvation in any other: for there is none other name under heaven given among men, whereby we must be saved.

13 Now when they saw the boldness of Peter and John, and perceived that they were unlearned and ignorant men, they marvelled; and they took knowledge of them, that they had been with Y**ah**U**shua**.

Acts 4:17-18 But that it spread no further among the people, let us straitly threaten them, that they speak henceforth to no man in this name.

18 And they called them, and commanded them not to speak at all nor teach in the name of Y**ah**U**shua**.

Acts 5:28-32 Saying, Did not we straitly command you that ye should not teach in this name? and, behold, ye have filled Jerusalem with your doctrine, and intend to bring this man's blood upon us.

29 Then Peter and the other apostles answered and said, We ought to obey **Elohim** rather than men.

30 The **Elohim** of our fathers raised up Y**ah**U**shua**, whom ye slew and hanged on a tree.

31 Him hath **Elohim** exalted with his right hand to be a Prince and a Saviour, for to give repentance to Israel, and forgiveness of sins.

32 And we are his witnesses of these things; and so is also the Ruach Ha Kodesh, whom **Elohim** hath given to them that obey him.

Acts 6:27-29 And when they had brought them, they set them before the council: and the high priest asked them,

28 Saying, Did not we straitly command you that ye should not teach in this name? and, behold, ye have filled Jerusalem with your doctrine, and intend to bring this man's blood upon us.

29 Then Peter and the other apostles answered and said, We ought to obey **Elohim** rather than men.

Acts 9:14-16 And here he hath authority from the chief priests to bind all that call on thy name.

15 But **YahUwah** said unto him, Go thy way: for he is a chosen vessel unto me, to bear my name before the Gentiles, and kings, and the children of Israel:

16 For I will shew him how great things he must suffer for my name's sake.

Acts 13:26 Menand brethren, children of the stock of Abraham, and whosoever among you **feareth _(i.e reverence)_** **Elohim**, to you is the word of this salvation sent.

Romans 9:17 For the scripture saith unto Pharaoh, Even for this same purpose have I raised thee up, that I might shew my power in thee, and that my name might be declared throughout all the earth.

Romans 10:12-14 For there is no difference between the Jew and the Greek: for the same **YahUwah** over all is rich unto all that call upon him.

13 For whosoever shall call upon the name of **YahUwah** shall be saved.

14 How then shall they call on him in whom they have not believed? and how shall they believe in him of whom they have not heard? and how shall they hear without a preacher?

Romans 1:16-17 For I am not ashamed of the evangel of the **Messiah**: for it is the power of **Elohim** unto salvation to every one that believeth; to the Jew first, and also to the Greek.

17 For therein is the righteousness of **Elohim** revealed from faith to faith: as it is written, The just shall live by faith.

1 Corinthians 12:2-3 Ye know that ye were Gentiles, carried away unto these dumb idols, even as ye were led.

3 Wherefore I give you to understand, that no man speaking by the Spirit of **Elohim** calleth Y*ah*Ushua accursed: and that no man can say that Y*ah*Ushua is Y*ah*Uwah, but by the Ruach Ha Kodesh.

1 Corinthians 15:33-34 Be not deceived: evil communications corrupt good manners.

34 Awake to righteousness, and sin not; for some have not the knowledge of **Elohim**: I speak this to your shame.

2 Timothy 2:15-16 Study to shew thyself approved unto **Elohim**, a workman that needeth not to be ashamed, rightly dividing the word of truth.

16 But **shun***(i.e. keep away from)***profane***(i.e. (by implication, of Jewish notions) heathenish)*and vain **babblings***(i.e. empty sounding, i.e. fruitless discussion)*: for they will **increase** *(i.e. to advance (in amount, to grow; in time, to be well along):--increase, proceed, profit, be far spent)* unto more wickedness.

2 Timothy 2:19 Nevertheless the foundation of **Elohim** standeth sure, having this seal, Y*ah*Uwah knoweth them that are his. And, let every one that nameth the name of the **Messiah** depart from iniquity.

1 Thessalonians 5:18-21 In every thing give thanks: for this is the will of **Elohim** in the **Messiah** Y*ah*Ushuaconcerning you.

19 Quench not the Spirit.

20 Despise not prophesyings.

21 **Prove** *(i.e. test (abstractly or concretely); by implication, trustiness:--experience(-riment), proof, trial)*all things; **hold** *(i.e. keep (in memory), let, X make toward, possess, retain, seize on, stay, take)*fast that which is good.

2 Thessalonians 1:7-8 And to you who are troubled rest with us, when Y_ah_U_wah_Y_ah_U_shua_ shall be revealed from heaven with his mighty malakhim,

8 In flaming fire taking vengeance on them that know not **Elohim**, and that obey not the evangel of our Y_ah_U_wah_Y_ah_U_shua_ the **Messiah**:

James 1:12 Blessed is the man that endureth temptation: for when he is tried, he shall receive the crown of life, which Y_ah_U_wah_ hath promised to them that **love _(i.e. agapao)_**him.

1 Peter 4:14, 16 If ye be reproached for the name of the **Messiah**, happy are ye; for the spirit of honor and of **Elohim** resteth upon you: on their part he is evil spoken of, but on your part he is magnified.

16 Yet if any man suffer as a Messianic, let him not be ashamed; but let him magnify **Elohim** on this behalf.

2 Peter 2:1 But there were false prophets also among the people, even as there shall be false teachers among you, who privily shall bring in damnable heresies, even **denying _(i.e. reject)_**Y_ah_U_wah_that bought them, and bring upon themselves swift destruction.

2 Peter 2:9 Y_ah_U_wah_knoweth how to deliver the righteous out of temptations, and to reserve the unjust unto the day of judgment to be punished:

2 Peter 2:14-15 Having eyes full of adultery, and that cannot cease from sin; beguiling unstable souls: an heart they have exercised with covetous practices; cursed children:

15 Which have forsaken the right way, and are gone astray, following the way of Balaam the son of Bosor, who loved the wages of unrighteousness;

1 John 2:21-23 I have not written unto you because ye know not the truth, but **because ye know it, and that no lie is of the truth.**

22 Who is a liar but he that denieth that Y_ah_U_shua_ is the **Messiah**? He is an **anti-messiah _(i.e. opponents against the Messiah)_**, that denieth the Father and the Son.

23 Whosoever denieth the Son, the same hath not the Father: he that acknowledgeth the Son hath the Father also.

1 John 3:22-24 And whatsoever we ask, we receive of him, because we keep his commandments, and do those things that are pleasing in his sight.

23 And this is his commandment, That we should believe on the name of his Son YAH**U**SHUA **the Messiah, and love _(i.e. agapao)_ one another, as he gave us commandment.**

24 And he that keepeth his commandments dwelleth in him, and he in him. And hereby we know that he abideth in us, by the Spirit which he hath given us.

1 John 5:13 These things have I written unto you that believe on the name of the Son of **Elohim**; that ye may know that ye have eternal life, and that ye may believe on the name of the Son of **Elohim**.

2 John 1:6-7 And this is **love _(i.e. agape)_**, that we walk after his commandments. This is the commandment, That, as ye have heard from the beginning, ye should walk in it.

7 For many deceivers are entered into the world, who confess not that Y**AH**U**SHUA** the **Messiah** is come in the flesh. This is a deceiver and **anti-messiah _(i.e. opponents against the Messiah)_**.

Revelation 3:8 I know thy works: behold, I have set before thee an open door, and no man can shut it: for thou hast a little strength, and hast kept my word, and hast not denied my name.

Revelation 11:18 And the nations were angry, and thy wrath is come, and the time of the dead, that they should be judged, and that thou shouldest give reward unto thy servants the prophets, and to the saints, and them that **fear _(i.e. reverence)_**thy name, small and great; and shouldest destroy them which destroy the earth.

Revelation 3:12 Him that overcometh will I make a pillar in the temple of my **Elohim**, and he shall go no more out: and I will write upon him the name of my **Elohim**, and the name of the city of my **Elohim**, which is new Jerusalem, which cometh down out of heaven from my **Elohim**: and I will write upon him my new name.

Revelation 14:12-13 Here is the patience of the saints: here are they that keep the commandments of **Elohim**, and the faith of Y**AH**U**SHUA**.

13 And I heard a voice from heaven saying unto me, Write, Blessed are the dead which die in Y**AH**U**WAH** from henceforth: Yea, saith the Spirit, that they may rest from their labours; and their works do follow them.

RESOURCE INFORMATION

King James Version
MOODY PRESS
Chicago, ILL.
Strong's Exhaustive Concordance
THOMAS NELSON PUBLISHERS
NASHVILLE, TENN.
SUN-DAY WORSHIP TERMS
COME OUT of HER MY PEOPLE
Institute for Scripture Research
8 Lark Street,
Rant en Dal,
Krugersdorp 1739
Republic of South Africa
The HTML Bible
PO Box31,
Elmwood, TN 38560
Kyran, Esq.
Assistant Counsel
www.gotquestions.org

www.ingramcontent.com/pod-product-compliance
Lightning Source LLC
Chambersburg PA
CBHW031546060726
47590CB00004BA/1530